TIME FOR KIDS READERS

A Family Music Shop

by Stephanie Buehler

Harcourt

SCHOOL PUBLISHERS

Orlando   Austin   New York   San Diego   Toronto   London

Visit *The Learning Site!*
www.harcourtschool.com

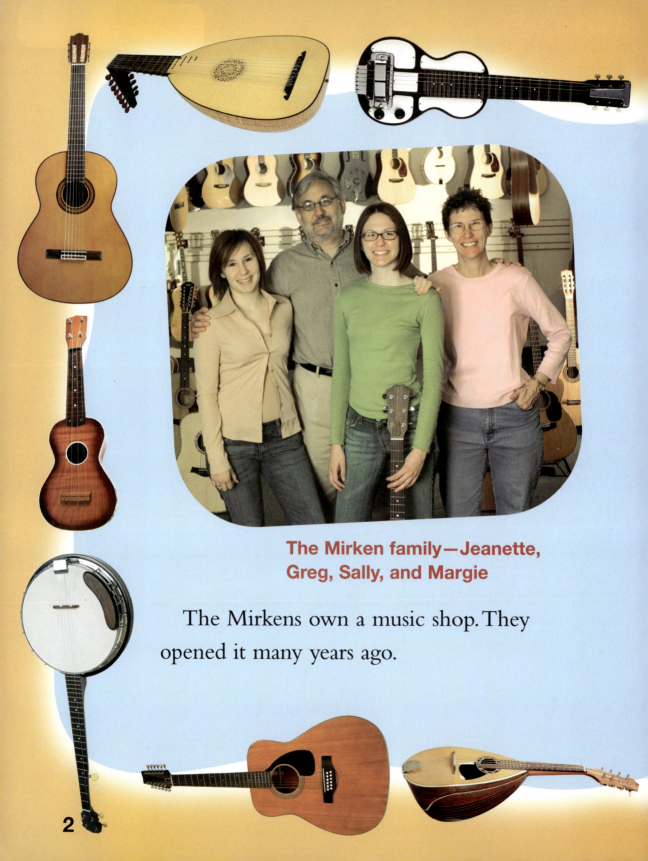

The Mirken family—Jeanette, Greg, Sally, and Margie

The Mirkens own a music shop. They opened it many years ago.

Margie shows a mandolin to a customer.

Greg and Margie work in the shop. Their daughters, Sally and Jeanette, work there, too.

3

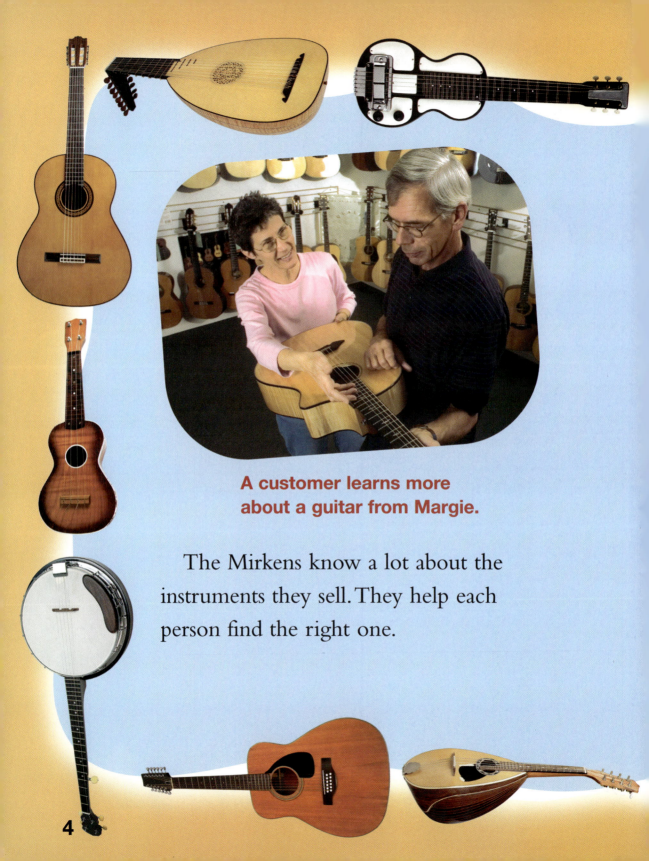

A customer learns more about a guitar from Margie.

The Mirkens know a lot about the instruments they sell. They help each person find the right one.

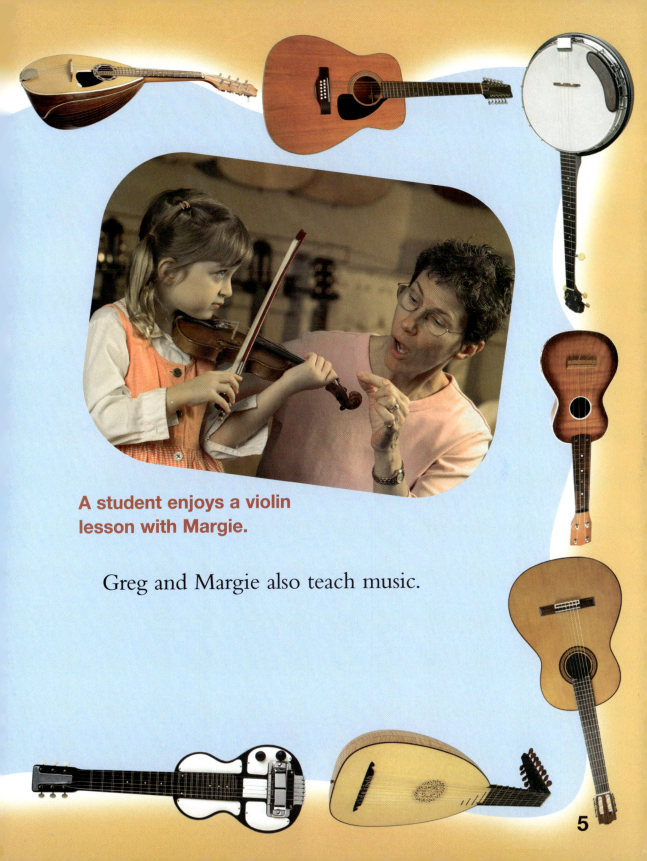

**A student enjoys a violin
lesson with Margie.**

Greg and Margie also teach music.

Sally helps her father fix a guitar.

Sometimes instruments get broken. People bring them to the Mirkens to be fixed.

6

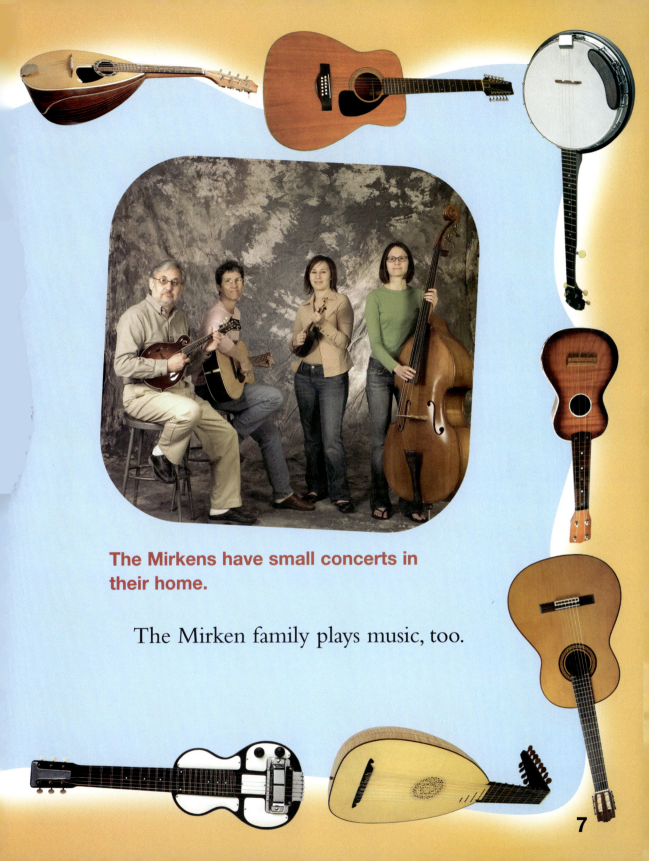

The Mirkens have small concerts in their home.

The Mirken family plays music, too.

The Mirkens are always ready to help a customer in their store.

"We treat people with respect," says Margie. That's why people like to shop there.